The Plot Mc

The PLOT MACHINE

Design Better Stories Faster

DALE KUTZERA

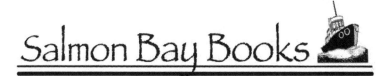

Salmon Bay Books

Contents

Introduction

Books on story structure typically describe the three-act framework and that's about it. They break stories down into traditional parts and sub-parts and present lists of necessary components. They may even reverse-engineer novels and movies to illustrate how structure has been successfully employed. This is great to a point, but reverse-engineering stories doesn't help you write your story.

What you need is a sequence of steps that takes you from blank page to working outline. What you need is a design process...a *Plot Machine*.

I use the word *design* because it is helpful to think of this process as separate from the act of writing. Let's say you crash on an alien planet. Your spaceship is wrecked, but several aliens pull you to safety and promise to build a house for you to live in.

Three things must happen. First, you must describe to the aliens what a house is and the function it serves to keep you warm and dry. Second, you have to understand the physical components of a house—floor, walls, roof, and doors—and how they are arranged. Lastly, you have to evaluate the materials on this strange planet and determine how they might be used to make a home. Perhaps some trees could be used for beams and some crystal for windows.

The process is the same in designing a story. You have to know what a story is and the function it serves in society. You need know the various components that comprise a traditional narrative: characters, situations, goals, obstacles, and themes.

And then you must evaluate the ideas you have and determine how they can be arranged in an overall design.

Is story design essential? Probably not. Many writers dive into prose with just a few story elements in place. They make their plots up on the fly, or by extensive editing after a mountain of prose has been written. There's nothing wrong with this process, but it isn't very efficient. And today's writer's, whether traditionally or independently published, recognize the importance of quantity as well as quality.

If you desire the rewards of building a large audience for your writing, then design skills will help you create a steady flow of stories. This guide is intended to help writers design better stories faster, resulting in cleaner first drafts and greater productivity.

This book starts off with an introduction to stories and their function in society. We will review a hierarchy of story-types and cover the general parameters of their design.

Part II begins the design process by assembling the major elements of a story. Part III introduces the traditional story structure upon which story elements are arranged. Part IV examines the challenging task of arranging parts into well-connected sequences. Part V presents a few case studies of using these design principles to break a handful of different story-types.

Story design is the art of arranging elements in a compelling order. Just as architects design a collection of volumes, writers design events and emotions. No guide can tell you what story to write or how to write it. Your personal artistry it the X-factor that only you can provide. A few coins in the plot machine, however, will provide options, perspective, and most important, a reliable process.

Let's get started.

PART 1

STORIES

The Stories We Tell

If you added up the amount of time human beings read books, watch TV and movies, go to the theater, or just chat around the water cooler, dinner table, or campfire, you may determine that telling stories is the primary human activity. Every society in every corner of the world tells stories.

Why are stories so central to human life?

Because they are our best survival skill.

We lack coats of fur, defensive horns, and sharp claws, but we have stories. For a hundred thousand years, homo sapiens have passed information through stories, myths, fables, and legends. They help us find food and mates, survive predators and natural disasters, and understand the world around us.

Those individuals that failed in this critical skill (Yes, I'm talking about you, Neanderthals!) were less likely to survive and procreate. You can, therefore, make a strong claim that modern humans evolved to be story-tellers and story-consumers. We seek stories just as we seek food and water.

In our modern world stories are more about entertainment than survival, but the primitive need they satisfy remains active in our dinosaur brains. Seen in this light, the value of any story is not in the story itself, but the information and wisdom it conveys to the consumer.

At its most basic form, a story is a recounting of events. It might be what you did at work, something that happened over the weekend, or what you did over summer vacation. Some stories are short, others long. Some merely recount unrelated events like a laundry list of items, while others present a sequence of related incidents that add up to some insightful conclusion.

This latter definition is what we typically mean when we talk about stories. Over the millennia, such stories have taken on a traditional structure and utilize a customary set of elements. While the means of telling a story have changed from spoken poems and plays to novels and motion pictures, the components of a story have changed little.

Stories still involve *characters* in a *difficult situation* undertaking a *great endeavor* to reach a *goal*.

These key elements define what we consider an effective story, one that appeals to a large audience, holds their interest, and provides lasting meaning even after the telling has ended. These are the kind of stories people pay good money to experience, and they are probably the kind of stories you want to design. To recap:

A *character or characters...*
in a *difficult situation...*
undertake an *endeavor...*
to reach a *goal*.

These elements are typically arranged into three main sections or acts.

Act 1: introduces the *characters* and their *situation*.
Act 2: sets them on the *endeavor*.
Act 3: depicts their success or failure to reach their *goal*.

Dividing a story into three acts goes back to the plays of ancient Greece and probably even further. The practice has been codified in countless screenwriting manuals. Readers are so accustomed to this story structure that many novelists have embraced it as a way to frame a story. It is the basis of most full-length novels, plays, operas, and motion pictures.

But this is just the broadest shape of a story and only presents the main elements a writer must assemble (*hero, situation, endeavor, goal*). Before we can begin the design process, we need a more specific understanding of the various types of stories we tell each other.

Story Taxonomy

A taxonomy is a fancy term for a means to categorize various things. Just as biologists classify animals into *Phylum, Class*, and *Order*, we can group stories according to *Motivation, Source,* and *Target*.

These divisions reflect the general human needs each type of story appeals to. In this regard, the range of stories reflects the human experience of living on Earth, encompassing our physical and emotional desires, our struggle for survival, and our yearning for a better life. Understanding these categories provides a solid foundation on which to build a story. Where your story-idea fits on the chart will influence how it is designed.

There is obviously some overlap in any hierarchy. Is a character battling a wild animal under *threat*, or *desiring* safety? Is a hero pursuing romance satisfying an *internal* or *external* desire? The exact divisions are not as important as a general understanding of the types of stories we tell. Let's take a look at each characteristic, starting with the most general division.

A Full Length Story

Act I

In which the hero is introduced
and a compelling need established.

Act II

In which the hero undertakes a unique
endeavor to achieve their goal.

Act III

In which the hero fails or succeeds.

Motivation: Threat or Desire?

The top layer of our taxonomy is *Motivation*. Just as everything on earth is either animal, vegetable or mineral, all stories can be divided into *Threat* or *Desire*. Either a character is under attack or they want something.

What *threats* and *desires* have in common is they place the main character in a compelling situation. The hero is either escaping a *threat* or pursuing a *desire*. Audiences can identify with the dramatic conflict inherent in either situation. A *threat* is something you must survive, and a desire is something difficult to obtain (if the *desire* was readily available, you'd have it already).

Threats and *desires* motivate the hero to undertake the challenge of Act II. The major distinction is that a *threat* is something impacting the hero, whereas a *desire* is something the hero is actively pursuing. One is reactive. The other is proactive. Threats imperil the hero's existing lifestyle, while desires hold the promise of improving his or her circumstances.

Source: External or Internal?

The next layer of division is the source of the motivation. Where is the *threat* coming from? What is the object of the hero's *desire*?

Threats can be divided into external and internal. Most are external, ranging from attacking animals to an approaching storm. For thousands of years, our ancestors gathered around campfires and traded stories of surviving external threats. Such stories offer life-saving insights. Today such stories play for entertainment, but they still appeal to our primal fight-or-flight instincts.

Internal Threats are less tangible and affect our physical or mental health. Illness and injury are universal perils. With

Story Taxonomy Chart

Motivation: Threat or Desire?

> Threat—something attacking hero
> Desire—something hero wants

Source: Internal or External?

> External Threats—War, Criminals, Fire
> Internal Threats—Disease, Trauma
> External Desire—Money, Food, Shelter
> Internal Desire—Love, Revenge, Honor

Target: General or Specific?

> General Threats—Storms, War
> Specific Threats—Blackmail, Vendetta
> General Desires—Peace, Prosperity
> Specific Desires—Treasure, a Mate

people living longer lives, old age and mental impairment are new variations of internal threats.

Desires can also be divided into external and internal objectives. The same ancient campfires witnessed tales of finding food, a mate, or a comfortable dwelling. Along with the invention of money came stories of finding treasure.

Internal desires are motivated by emotional or intellectual needs. Detectives pursue criminals out of a sense of justice. Soldiers volunteer out of patriotism. A victim may pursue a tormentor driven by vengeance.

Target: Individual or Shared?

The third category divides stories into those affecting just the hero and those affecting a larger community.

External Threats can target the hero alone or threaten the hero's village. Likewise, an *Internal Threat* can afflict only the hero (a broken leg) or present a more general threat (a plague or virus).

Desires can also be specific to the hero or shared by the larger community. Finding true love typically benefits just the hero. Winning a war or bringing rain to a parched land benefits everyone. The number of characters benefiting is an aspect of scale, a design parameter we will explore shortly.

This story taxonomy could be extended into ever more specific categories. For example, *External Threats* could be divided into categories like *Acts of Nature* (storms), *Wild Animals* (shark), or *Acts of Humankind* (war). Further division would be redundant for our purposes. What is important to note is the variety of *Threats* and *Desires* and the resulting motivation that will drive your character through the second act of your story.

Design Guides

In any design task there are general conventions that guide the process. Before architects puts pencil to paper, they know the type of building they're designing, the budget, the characteristics of the building site, and any restrictions imposed by zoning codes.

Before designing a story, a writer should take a moment to understand a few guiding principles. Arranging the elements of a story can be difficult or agonizing (it's seldom easy), and design guides can help frame the process.

Entertainment Value

It may seem crass to talk about the entertainment value of a story, but the hard reality is a story's appeal is based on the quality and quantity of entertainment it delivers.

At its most basic level, entertainment is the release of tension. A predicament establishes tension and the resolution provides release. A man walking a tightrope creates tension. Reaching the far end safely provides the release.

What is entertaining varies over time and cultures, but boils down to *emotions, action, information, physical feats*, and *spectacle*. These elements can exist on their own. Vaudeville was based on a series of acts—dancing bear, comedian, juggler, singer—that were entertaining on their own, but had no narrative connection.

You may have some entertaining elements of your story in mind, but don't fall in love with them at this point. Doing so can tempt you to gerrymander the plot to accommodate a favorite set-piece. Instead, keep in mind the entertainment opportunities of a given story-type and allow room for the hijinx that will be specified later.

Scale

Stories can be small and contained or large and sprawling. Contained stories are easier to design and appeal to a broader audience as their entertainment value is conveyed in a compact form. A sprawling story typically involves more people, complex motivations, and a more elaborate structure. Such stories demands a greater investment in time and attention by the writer and the audience.

Your story may lend itself to different scales. A crime story may unfold in one city in a few days. A fantasy epic could span centuries and solar systems. Private Investigators typically work in one town, but a secret agent is expected to travel the globe.

In addition to time and locations, scale can be measured by the number of characters and plot lines. Romances, soap operas, and historical dramas often explore a single location through a variety of characters and plots.

Almost any story-type can be adjusted in scale. Sometimes boiling down an idea can heighten the dramatic impact by removing extraneous elements. Conversely, expanding the scope can broaden the spectrum of emotions and deepen the experience.

Ask yourself how much time passes in the course of your story, particularly in the second act. Hours? Days? Years? Consider how much physical space your characters inhabit. One room? A city? Various planets?

Tone

Where *scale* involves the range of time and space in your story, *tone* reflects the range from *reality* to *fantasy*. This spectrum has nothing to do with genre. Comedies can range from realistic to screwball. Some science-fiction is tough and gritty while many contemporary stories are fantastical.

Common Entertainment Values

Emotions
Poetry
Music
Comedy
Beautiful or terrifying scenery

Physical Conflict
Fights
Chases
Epic battles

Information
Puzzles and Riddles
Secrets revealed

Physical Feats
Sports
Races
Acrobatics

Spectacle
Explosions or Fireworks
Natural disasters

The tonal spectrum can be described as the real-world relationship between cause and effect. When a character is knocked on the head, do they bleed or do they roll their eyes and see little birds? Children's stories and comedies lean toward the fantastic end of the spectrum. Drama, particularly tragedies, lean toward the realistic.

Where your story fits on the tonal spectrum will influence what kind of scenes are plausible in your particular universe. A pie-fight that is appropriate in a comedy would be out of place in a gritty crime drama.

Theme

We know that the best stories provide life-lessons that have lasting meaning. These are expressed as the theme of your story.

Traditional story structure presents a hero that embodies a universal human frailty. Their attempt to reach their goal initially fails due to this frailty and only after they have recognized and corrected their flaw can they reach their goal.

At the broadest level, all themes are about achieving balance. The hero finds balance by gaining what he lacks or giving up what he has too much of. As the audience experiences the story through the hero, they also appreciate what aspects of their own lives are out of balance. This thematic equation informs the events of Act III.

Popular Character Arcs/Themes

Start   ### End

From Dishonest   To Honest
From Lone Wolf   To Team Player
From Traumatized   To Healed
From Naive   To Worldly
From Peacemaker   To Warrior
From Impulsive   To Thoughtful
From Bitter   To Forgiving
From Selfish   To Selfless
From Timid   To Bold
From Intellectual   To Emotional

PART TWO

ELEMENTS

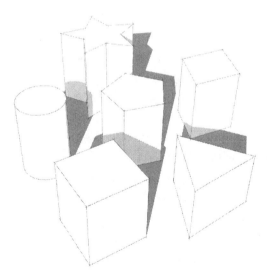

The Parts
of a Story

Stories are comprised of various elements: characters, settings, situations, themes, and so on. Some elements burst into the writer's imagination effortlessly, others require conscious thought and trial and error. You may already have a variety of elements in mind, but it's important to focus on the main elements of your story.

Don't start with Act I. The most important elements are those that fill Act II and III. You may wonder how the second act can be designed without knowing what happens in the first act. Look at it this way: Act I merely sets the table for the feast of Act II, and you won't know what dishes to put on the table until you know what food is being served.

You can find many story elements by exploring the logical extensions of the elements that first sparked your imagination. In this way, assembling the main parts of your story is a process of asking the right questions in the right order.

Question One:
What do you have?

Chances are something popped into your imagination and you thought, "Hey, that would make a great story!" It was most likely a *Character, Setting, Situation,* or *Genre*. This is the seed from which your story grows. The great thing about a seed is it holds the DNA of the plant it will become.

Some story elements naturally relate to others. For example, a genre can imply a setting such as the gritty city of a crime story. A setting is naturally filled with certain types of characters. For example, hospitals often have overworked nurses and egomaniacal doctors. In turn, characters can imply goals: detectives want to catch bad guys.

The design process starts by exploring what you have. What drew you to this idea? Why has it captivated your imagination? Why would it make a great story? What is compelling about this setting or character? What entertainment value does a particular genre or situation promise?

Explore what you have. Make a list.

The objective is to identify the main components of *character, endeavor,* and *goal*.

Remember that you have the grand storytelling tradition to draw upon. It's your job to meet the expectations of a given genre, exceed them, and twist them in surprising ways.

You also have your own writing skills and tastes to consider. What sort of scenes are you comfortable writing? Are you great with action? Do you loathe dialogue? What genre do you love and know deeply? Keep your strengths, weaknesses, and passions in mind as you make your list of elements. By studying what you have, you will also learn what you don't have and must find.

Question Two:
What is the hero's goal?

Often the goal stems naturally from whatever element first sparked your imagination. The POW planning an escape is seeking freedom. The cop going undercover is trying to trap a criminal. The romantic hero on a quest is trying to win the hand of a lover. In the best of situations, the goal flows naturally from the other elements you have set in place.

The key relationship to keep in mind is that the goal must be worth the torment the hero endures in Act II. If the *endeavor* is extreme (and it should be), then it may be difficult to devise a goal that justifies it. And the *endeavor* must be justified or the audience will question your hero's sanity (and the writer's talent).

Where your story fits on the taxonomy chart will also indicate what your hero's goal is. *Threat* stories have a general goal of safety, but this can be achieved in different ways. A dragon may need to be slain, but an approaching tsunami implies a goal of reaching higher ground.

If the *desire* is love, then the goal comes in the form of a potential mate. Intangible desires such as freedom or vengeance are best symbolized in some tangible form. A detective may dream of personally putting the elusive Mr. Big behind bars. Let's look at four common goals.

Treasure

The simplest goal is treasure. Nothing stirs a reader's imagination more than a buried treasure. Of course, treasure can come in a variety of forms: gold, a secret formula, proof of one's innocence. What these things have in common is that the hero lacks them in the first act and needs them so badly they will endure the tribulations of the second act.

Common Starting Elements

Characters
Lover
Warrior
Fool
Introvert

Settings
Contemporary
Historical
Fantasy

Situation
A new power or wealth
Facing a great challenge
Going into battle
Finding a killer

Goal
The love of another
A great treasure
Vengeance
Accomplishing an impossible feat

Genre
Romance
Crime
Mystery
Thriller
Science Fiction

Safety

In stories of survival, the hero's normal world is threatened by a storm, invading army, or some other antagonistic force. Sometimes the force can be opposed. A lion attacking a village can be hunted and killed, but you can't kill a typhoon or a volcano. All you can do is escape it. In such situations, safety is made tangible by a geographic destination. Perhaps it is high ground, or a different island, or a storm cellar.

Personal Achievement

We all desire achievement. Very few of us are content with our present circumstances. We are drawn to stories involving a hero determined to prove they are more than they appear to be. Such stories present the hero with an opportunity to prove themselves. This typically is a chance to demonstrate a talent—performance, athletics, intellectual ability—in a public venue.

Emotional Wholeness

Even the most content human beings may feel out of balance. Their creature comforts have been satisfied, but their soul aches. Emotional wholeness can set a hero on a more internal quest. The goal itself can be elusive. They'll know it only when they find it. In such stories the goal is identified and defined through the act of searching for it.

If you start with a character or genre, the goal may be self-evident. If you start with a situation, ask yourself if it would naturally lead a hero to seek a desire or safety. If you start with a specific kind of treasure, ask yourself who would want it, and prepare to place it well out of their reach. If you start with a setting, explore the people who live there, and likely situations they encounter.

Question Three:
What is your Endeavor?

The most important element your story is the *endeavor*. In the modern world of high-concept storytelling, the *endeavor* is what drives audiences into theaters and bookstores. Even the hero's ultimate goal takes a back seat to the manner in which they overcome obstacles to achieve it.

You may have locked in on a hero, but set that character aside for now. It is best to define their *endeavor* first. Compelling endeavors make compelling characters, but a tepid endeavor can make even the most interesting character dull and pedestrian.

You may also have a general goal. For now, keep it that way. A general goal helps design the endeavor, but the endeavor itself may require adjusting the specifics of the goal.

Fortunately, there are only a handful of ways human beings reach goals, so there are only a handful of endeavor types. These endeavors can work in any story though some are closely associated with specific genres. Thrillers and crime stories often involve a *quest*. Romances often involve *subterfuge*.

Consider different options and choose one that best sustains your second act with conflict and entertainment. Keep in mind that some stories require only one endeavor while others may employ a handful (hero on a *quest* may be captured and need to *escape*). At this point focus on the main endeavor. Lets examine each type one at a time.

A Quest

The *quest* is a classic endeavor. *The Odyssey, Canterbury Tales*, and *Don Quixote* are all quest stories. So are *Lord of the Rings, Star Wars*, and the *James Bond* movies. Perhaps a quest strikes some universal human need to explore what lies beyond the mountains or over an ocean. They appeal to our curiosity and restless nature.

The entertainment value of a quest story lies in the new environments visited along the way. Landscapes, cities, and cultures all provide visual spectacle and potential danger. Quests need not span continents. Exploring the dark underbelly of a small town is a kind of quest. The hero's goal could be to obtain something, deliver something, warn someone of a pending danger, or perform a task as a test of their skill and bravery.

Storm the Castle

If the hero's goal is guarded by layers of defenses, they must *storm the castle* to reach it. This story type focuses the activity of the second act around one guarded location. The writer can invent as many obstacles as they wish. A short story could involve simply a tall wall to climb over. A feature film could involve guards, a moat, motion-sensor alarms, laser beam triggers, and guard dogs. The potential weakness of this endeavor is that it can become repetitive.

These hurdles may be known to the hero before they embark on the endeavor. There may be a scene in which each is listed, conveying to the audience the difficulty of the task they are about to witness.

Subterfuge

A *subterfuge* endeavor has the hero take on a different persona to obtain their goal. The entertainment value comes from watching a person struggle to be something very different from their true selves. Changing occupations, races, sexes, or social classes is often played to comedic effect. Such an endeavor typically requires a significant goal to lead the hero into this desperate situation. These stories generally utilize a broad, farcical tone.

Escape

An *escape* endeavor is the opposite of *storm the castle*. The hero is trapped in a location or a desperate situation and must find a way out. Many prison dramas are based on planning and executing an escape. War dramas may involve a squad of soldiers trapped behind enemy lines. The situation need not involve physical confinement. A family drama could involve a hero trapped in an unpleasant marriage. A thriller may involve a hero who is mistaken for a criminal and must prove his true identity.

The great thing about escape endeavors is that the goal is inherent to the situation. Very little motivation is needed to explain why a POW wants to dig a tunnel under the barbed wire fence.

Prepare for Battle

Preparation is part of almost every story, but sometimes it can be the primary endeavor. Consider the boxer preparing for a title match, or the lawyer preparing for a big case. There is less conflict in such endeavors as the hero is typically not engaged in head-to-head competition with the opponent until Act III. The writer must layer on the internal and external complications through Act II so that the climax carries multiple impacts. Losing the boxing match may mean losing a romance. An acquittal might wreck a lawyer's career.

Empowered

Who wouldn't like super powers? It is an ancient human desire. We'd all like to fly, read minds, seduce lovers, or travel back in time. Many stories involve characters imbued with new powers. These could be fantastical or based in reality. Inheriting a fortune from a long-lost relative grants the power of wealth. Being cured of a debilitating disease is to gain the power of health. The entertainment value of such stories lies in the vicarious thrill the audience has in experiencing these new powers.

Episodic

Some stories ignore structural paradigms and merely engage the hero in a series of loosely connected episodes. Comedies often employ this loose framework in order to present various gags and set-pieces. Such stories typically entertain in the moment, but have little lasting meaning or universal theme.

Given the different elements you have, try on different endeavors. In some genres, the endeavor is self-evident. Detectives and dragon-slayers go on quests. If your story started with a situation, that may also define your endeavor. Take a moment to consider alternatives. Be open to alter your goal if required. Nothing is set in stone.

Question Four:
Who is Your Hero?

You may have thought this is where the design process starts. After all, isn't the hero the most important element of your story? Well, yes and no. A compelling, sympathetic hero is vital, but heroes are only made compelling and sympathetic by the *goals* they have and the *endeavors* they endure to obtain them.

By waiting until we have the other key elements in place, we can efficiently devise the perfect hero to inhabit them. For example, the goal tells us a lot about our hero. A romantic goal means our hero is lacking in love or unhappy in their current relationship. The goal of treasure implies a poor hero. If the goal is escaping prison, then the hero's backstory involves a crime that put him behind bars.

The hero must be physically and mentally capable of surviving the *endeavor*. Great endeavors, therefore, require great abilities. Some heroes may have these skills while others need to go through training.

Your hero must also be logically motivated to undergo the *endeavor*. In the simplest situations, their motivation is linked to their occupation. Cops investigate crimes. Secret agents fight maniacal villains. Doctors and nurses heal people. No further motivation is needed.

More challenging are stories in which your hero has no organic motivation. They must be pushed to undertake the travails of Act II and there must be no logical alternative. If there is a logical alternative, they must attempt it and be foiled. The *endeavor* can be their only course of action.

Here are the common hero types:

The Righteous Hero

Many myths and fables involve a righteous hero who seeks to correct any wrong he or she encounters. This character is attractive, physically fit, and morally incorruptible. They represent an ideal of human character. Their constancy and reliability are comforting, even if their lack of flaws make them hard to identify with.

The Unskilled Hero

A more relatable hero is one who seems ill-suited to the task at hand. They are neither good-looking nor prime physical specimens. They may not be the brightest bulb in the lamp, and may have a loose grip on their moral compass. They are, in essence, more like us. They may go on the adventure of Act II kicking and screaming. The benefits of such a hero are their sympathetic and relatable qualities.

The Rogue

Some hero's have less than honorable motivations. They are in it for themselves. Though greed and self-centeredness are negative qualities, everyone can recognize them. Perhaps there are valid reasons for this hero's darker qualities. They often carry the emotional baggage of a troubled past. The emotional reward of such a character is seeing them grow beyond their lone-wolf status to embrace a larger sense of self-worth and community involvement.

The Tormented Hero

Some folks can never catch a break. They are trapped in an apparently endless cycle of misery. They are orphans, unloved, cast out, and downtrodden. The rest of the tribe makes fun of them, burdens them with the toughest jobs, or ignores their misery completely. Such heroes may have given up on themselves. They may believe their fate is beyond their control. The entertainment value of such a hero is their own dawning realization of their true worth.

Given your *endeavor* and *goal*, try on different types of heroes. How would a righteous hero behave differently through the second act than a rogue? What sort of hero would require the most dramatic character arc to survive the endeavor? Would a tormented hero spark the most entertainment value? Mix and match endeavors and heros. You can always change your mind later.

PART THREE

STRUCTURE

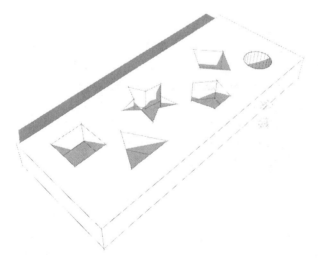

The Framework
of a story

By now you have a few key story elements in hand. You know the type of story your writing, the general goal and type of endeavor and hero. Let's set these elements aside and study the framework in which they are typically arranged.

Structure is an often-maligned word in the storytelling industry. It conjures images of crass hacks, paid by the word, banging out pulp stories. Even the most high-brow of literary lions, however, employs structure whether consciously or not. And many of those pulp hacks wrote great stories we still cherish decades later.

Structure is just a tool—one understood by billions of story-consumers around the world. What really matters is how you use this tool.

It is tempting to start at the beginning of Act I, but try not to think of a story as scenes stacked one after another. Think of it as one thing designed from general to specific. After all, architects do not start their work by designing the front door of a building and proceeding to the entry and then subsequent rooms. They treat a building as a general arrangements of elements before considering each component in greater detail. Likewise, we should look at the framework of story from general to specific.

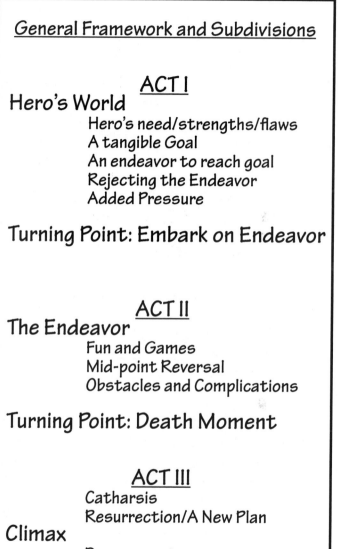

General Framework and Subdivisions

ACT I
Hero's World
- Hero's need/strengths/flaws
- A tangible Goal
- An endeavor to reach goal
- Rejecting the Endeavor
- Added Pressure

Turning Point: Embark on Endeavor

ACT II
The Endeavor
- Fun and Games
- Mid-point Reversal
- Obstacles and Complications

Turning Point: Death Moment

ACT III
- Catharsis
- Resurrection/A New Plan

Climax
- Denouement

The General Framework

We know that story elements are typically arranged into a beginning, middle, and end. These are roughly defined as three acts. It follows that between these acts there are two transitions, often called turning points or plot points.

Let's look at the main parts of the framework. We will start with Act II because the *endeavor* is the most important part of your story and everything flows from it.

Act II

This is where the hero engages in the *endeavor*.

Second Turning Point

This is often referred to as the *Death Moment* where the hero's failure is apparently complete.

Act III

Somehow the hero recovers from the defeat and redoubles his/her efforts to reach the goal. This act includes the final *climax* where the hero succeeds or fails.

Act I

The contents of Act II and III define Act I. This is where the hero is introduced and his need established, a need that will motivate him to take on the *endeavor* to reach the *goal*.

First Turning Point

The hero undertakes the *endeavor*. They start their quest, adopt their new identity, or are imbued with new powers.

These acts and turning points make up the broad sweeps of your story. Using your particular story elements, you should be able to fill the blanks of the following sentence:

> A hero who currently *(normal world)*, requires *(goal)* and decides to *(endeavor)*, leading him to *(climax)*.

Framework Subdivisions

As you can see, the general framework of a story is fairly simple. We can further break down the framework into a handful of subdivisions. As always, it is helpful to start with the middle-part of the story:

ACT II

We know that Act II contains the *endeavor*, but we also know endeavors can come in several shapes and sizes. A *subterfuge* story may lend itself to a different framework than a *storm the castle* story. Subdivisions can break the second act into more manageable chunks.

Fun and Games

There is often an upbeat quality to the first part of Act II. For example, going on a *quest* is exciting. New lands are explored. New people and creatures met, some of whom may become allies or traitors. The stakes are not terribly high right now and there is still time to turn back and call the whole thing off.

This is often called the *fun and games*, or *hijinx* part of a story and is where much of the entertainment value of a premise is delivered. A superhero uses his new powers. A hero in disguise experiences comic misunderstandings. A hero going to war bonds with fellow soldiers.

Mid-Point Reversal

Fun and Games are often insufficient to sustain a feature-length story. Once the obvious gags have been played out, the audience wants something fresh and different. The story has to take a turn.

This turn is often from positive to negative. A detective chasing a bad guy may learn he has become the killer's target. Those on a road-trip encounter obstacles and consider going back. A superhero learns his new powers come with responsibilities he'd rather not bear.

The *mid-point reversal* may also be where the hero goes from reactive to proactive. New dramatic possibilities within the same situation are sparked by reversing the dynamics that sustained the first part of Act II. A character being chased may turn the tables and go on the offensive or vice versa. Instead of merely surviving the alien invasion, they decide to fight the alien army. This can be a very satisfying turn.

Not all stories require a *mid-point reversal. Storm the Castle* and *Escape* stories have goals that carry through Act II and the hero's objective remains consistent.

Death Moment

Classic story structure ends Act II with the hero near death or complete failure. A detective not only fails to solve a crime, but wrecks his/her career. A lover fails to win their ideal mate and settles for a clearly flawed companion. The hero angers the dragon and it attacks the village.

Audiences consume stories to experience thrills, love, joy, and wonder. The *Death Moment* marks the low end of the emotional spectrum. One reason to start the design process with Act II is that an effective *death moment* will define what elements must be established in Act I.

POPULAR MID-POINT REVERSALS

Hero obtains a treasure and is now chased
Hero on the defense goes on offense
Hero realizes new power is a burden
Hero escapes but must free others
Detective makes arrest...wants conviction
Hero learns he was set up as a fall-guy
Hero wins goal, but must hide subterfuge

POPULAR DEATH MOMENTS

The hero dies and must be resuscitated
The hero is wounded and out of action
The endeavor has failed miserably
The hero is fired from his job
The couple breaks up their romance
The wedding is called off
The hero is mocked by his peers
The ideal mate marries someone else
The villain reaches their destination
The treasure is lost
A key ally is killed

ACT III

The bar is high in designing the third act. Many story elements come into sharp conclusion in rapid succession. Both external action and internal psychology are quickly churning, leaving the audience breathless and exhilarated. Fortunately, the third act can also be sub-divided into more manageable parts. Third acts are tricky, but their precise execution is vital to the structural integrity of a story.

If a story has any universal meaning it is delivered in its resolution. Such deeper resonance is not entirely needed. Plenty of stories deliver their entertainment value and that's all. This sums up a lot of crime and comedy stories. They come and go with little lasting resonance. A well-designed ending, however, can stand the test of time.

Catharsis

If the *death moment* ends the second act, then the *catharsis* begins the third. This is where the hero recognizes some internal flaw within themselves. Only by realizing this flaw contributed to their apparent failure can they transcend that weakness and ultimately succeed. They may need to apologize to those they've wronged and ask for forgiveness. They may also need to repair relationships or let others take the lead.

Resurrection/New Plan

A story could end with the hero failing to reach their goal, but wiser for the act of trying. Audiences prefer a winner, however, and like to see a hero rise from the ashes of defeat.

The *resurrection* typically happens right on the heels of the *catharsis*. Armed with a new awareness of their flaws, the hero is presented with a new opportunity to reach their goal. This could be a different endeavor or a variation on the endeavor that failed.

POSITIVE CATHARSIS MOMENTS
The hero learns to...
trust others.
be a team player
accept his real self
not hide behind a mask
let others shine
not take shortcuts
play by the rules
grow up and act his/her age
take responsibility for actions

NEGATIVE CATHARSIS MOMENTS
The hero learns to...
play outside the rules.
fight fire with fire.
use trickery and subterfuge.
show no mercy
risk everything

POPULAR RESURRECTION / NEW PLANS
The hero finds...
a means to heal his wounds
an alternative weapon to use
a means to reach the villain in time
a message with new information
a new witness
a new map
a key to escape captivity
inspiration in a pep-talk from an ally
inspiration from an ally's sacrifice

Climax

Finally, the hero engages the villain and is victorious or defeated. Audiences have a great deal of experience with climaxes. No matter how great the physical action, we're certain the hero will win because they have rejected their flaws and embraced positive human qualities.

Denouement

Following the excitement of the *endeavor* and *climax*, the audience craves a reward. They want the hero to relish in their victory, to see lovers kiss and walk down the aisle, and to witness the villain put into chains and locked away. We want to know things are right in the world, that evil is punished and virtue rewarded. The denouement holds all these things.

This section of a story needn't be lengthy. Sometimes just a glance between characters is enough convey "happily ever after." Often the denouement acts as a bookend to events in Act I. The hero's day-to-day life is mirrored with telling differences based on the new skills they have learned and the rewards they have earned.

Denouements also have the practical function of wrapping up loose ends, buttoning up sub-plots, and acting as a palate-cleanser for the audience as they prepare to leave the world of the story behind. With the current popularity of writing in series, the *denouement* may also set up some unfinished issues or introduce a new challenge that the hero will face in the next installment.

ACT I

Because you started the design process with Act II and III, you now have a list of elements to set up in Act I. These elements can be conveyed via a handful of common components. Not all of these items need to be used. In fact, a modern trend

POPULAR DENOUEMENTS

A wedding
A public declaration of love
The hero welcomed home
An award ceremony
The hero spending the treasure
The hero helping his allies
The hero at peace with himself
Hero helps others with similar challenges
The hero honoring fallen comrades
The hero retiring from her job
The villain suffering in defeat
The villain punished
The villain vowing revenge

in writing is to condense or do away with Act I in order to get to the fun of Act II as quickly as possible.

Prologue

Some stories require the audience to understand complex circumstances before a story begins. Perhaps the political history of a fantasy realm must be conveyed. A *prologue* is an acceptable way of conveying such tedious information.

Often prologues are used to start a story with action. If your hero's normal life is not very exciting, consider a prologue that introduces the villain in action. Even if we don't see the villain again in the rest of Act I, this will build anticipation for the inevitable conflict between villain and hero.

Action and information can also be conveyed through a prologue flashback to a fight in the hero's past, or a flashforward to a desperate moment from later in the story.

Opening Action

One sure-fire story-telling technique is to start off with action. Such scenes require no background information. We don't need to know where we are or who the character are. The conflict itself grabs our attention and we forget our own lives and focus on the story.

A fight will certainly establish tension. It could be a playground fight between two students or an epic space battle. A secret agent may be wrapping up a dangerous assignment or a superhero could be saving the planet. The appeal is the danger involved and our interest in who wins.

Even passive heroes should also be introduced in a moment of conflict. Intellectual battles can work, even if they are less visually striking. This could be an exam, a verbal argument, or a public performance. Perhaps a despotic boss dumps a fresh load of work on the hero's desk.

Whatever the conflict, the opening Action should introduce the relevant qualities of our hero and may mirror how they perform in the *death moment* and the *climax*. A failure in this opening scene can endear the hero to the audience.

The Hero's World

Typically the hero is introduced as they go about their day-to-day activities. That is not to say these activities are dull. Active heroes, like police officers, may be stalking a criminal. The everyday world may be a polar opposite from the world of Act II. This is most evident in fish-out-of-water stories based on the conflict between hero and setting.

Empowered stories present the pre-empowered hero. In such cases there can be a set-up/pay-off relationship between their day-to-day struggles without powers and how they deal with the same situations with their new powers.

In this regard, Act II further serves to define Act I. In *desire* stories, the hero lacks in Act I what they are trying to achieve in Act II. In *threat* stories, the hero possesses in Act I that which is threatened in Act II.

The age-old mantra of show don't tell is important here. The hero's normal world must be conveyed through happening events, not a recitation of facts. They should be pursuing a goal that introduces their world, occupation, ongoing conflicts, and underlying needs. This goal can relate to their need. If they are need love, they might be going on blind dates. If they need treasure, they might be asking for a raise.

The Villain's World

In stories where the hero is trying to stop a villain's plan, the villain may need their own first act. This leads to an interleaving of scenes involving the hero and villain separately, all leading to the initiation of their direct conflict in Act II.

Villains may require motivation to engage in their own endeavor. Such motivations are often based on negative traits like greed or envy. Your villain may merit their own need and motivation. Such complexities require more patience and attention on the part of the writer and the audience, but can present a more nuanced villain.

One important consideration is the audience's anticipation of the coming conflict. Even if your story is of the slow-burn variety, the first act should relate to the central endeavor. Nothing focuses a sailor's attention like storm clouds on the horizon. The same feeling of pending danger will keep readers turning pages.

The Inciting Incident

Into every life, some rain must fall. Into the hero's world, an *inciting incident* must happen. This incident typically presents a solution to the hero's established need. A hero looking for love may bump into the most beautiful mate he/she has ever seen. A hero in need of money may stumble across a treasure map.

Events can also intrude upon perfectly content heroes. A reformed thief could be visited by a past criminal associate. A village may be attacked by a dragon.

The inciting incident is typically where the hero's general *need* meets their specific *goal*. The means to reach this goal—the *endeavor*—may not yet be evident.

Rejecting the Endeavor

For active heroes, the *goal* and *endeavor* are often part of their job. A detective wants to arrest the murderer. Soldiers want to take the high ground. Surgeons eagerly take on the most challenging cases.

Less active heroes understandably shy away from what

may be the most dangerous adventure in their lives. This moment is typically called *rejecting the call to action*.

Instead of diving in to the endeavor, these heroes explore logical alternatives. For example, a hero in need of money may attempt to get a bank loan before they rob a bank. They might seek a raise at work or beg relatives for a loan. Of course, none of this works, but all common alternatives should be explored and checked off. Logic demands it.

Added Pressure

For heroes who initially reject the endeavor, additional pressure may be needed to force them to action. The poor man's bills pile up and he's being evicted. The lonely woman suffers through another New Years party, the only one not kissed at midnight. The dragon attacks the village again.

Pressure can come from any or all facets of a character's life: family, career, or personal identity. Often such pressure is conveyed through B- and C-stories that weave in and out of the main A story. Avoid tired, shopworn motivators like the clichéd *sick relative who needs an operation*.

In addition to sparking action, added pressure can establish a ticking clock. This puts pressure on the hero and conveys the time-scale of the story. People like knowing where a story is going and how long it will take to get there.

With these subdivisions in hand, you should be able to fill in the blanks of the following generic framework:

> *A hero who currently (normal world), goes about his life using his (strengths) but is hampered by his (flaws). He requires (goal) and might undertake (endeavor), but rejects it as too risky. One day (added pressure) happens, forcing his hand. He embarks on*

the (endeavor) and marvels at the (fun and games). While his (strengths) serve him well, his (flaws) lead him to (death moment). He realizes the error of his ways when (catharsis), but believes he can still reach his goal by (new plan). Using his (new skills) he engages in (climax). With victory in hand, the hero is rewarded with a (denouement).

Framework Variations

The exact framework of your story depends largely on your genre and your hero's particular *endeavor*. Just as the steel frame of a hospital is different from that of a office building, the frame of your story varies according to its content. Several standard variations are possible for the *endeavor* and *climax*. There are fewer set variations for Act I, perhaps one reason they are so easy to write.

ENDEAVOR VARIATIONS

Obstacles

The simplest type of *endeavor* has one hero battling various obstacles to reach his or her goal. Think of obstacles as *stuff in the hero's way*. The number of obstacles depends on the length of your story. A short story may require only a few where a full-length story may need a dozen or more.

Some vengeance stories involve a wronged hero battling through layers of obstacles to reach the person that hurt them. A sports story may fill Act II with qualifying competitions before the climactic national championship. Thieves robbing a bank may have to pass through layers of defenses.

POPULAR OBSTACLES

The early rounds of a tournament
Various henchmen guarding Mr. Big
Layers of defenses
Bad weather
Unreliable transportation

POPULAR SHIFTING GOALS

To reach their primary goal, the hero must:
Secure a weapon
Locate a map
Obtain a key or pass code
Enlist allies
Pinpoint a location
Win an endorsement
Travel a great distance
Find a witness
Convey a message
Escape from a trap

POPULAR COMPLICATIONS

A traitor in their midst
A rival for the goal
False leads and red herrings
Attacks by henchmen or rivals
A wounded ally
Arrested by authorities

Shifting Goals

Obstacles are evident in many stories, but may not be enough to sustain a narrative. The addition of shifting goals can enrich the plot, further explore the setting, and test your hero in different ways.

Here's an example of *shifting goals*: To win the hand of a maiden, a hero must prove his worthiness by slaying a dragon. To do that, the hero needs a special weapon. This weapon is held in guarded castle. A team of allies is needed to steal it. A ship is needed for their journey.

As you can see, the goal shifts from winning the maiden to securing a ship to take a team to steal a weapon and kill a dragon. The primary goal is the maiden, but that is quickly submerged by subordinate goals.

Even here, nothing is easy for the hero. Each subordinate goal should be saddled with frustrating complications. The dragon is invincible. The weapon is locked up. The allies are drunken scoundrels. The ship is a leaky rust-bucket.

In stories where the hero's goal is to stop the villain, the writer must design the villain's primary and subordinate goals. For instance, a super-villain may need various parts to assemble a devastating weapon. Each of the villain's sub-goals then presents a related sub-goal for the hero.

Subplots

Another alternative for Act II is to include two or three significant subplots. In this type of story, the primary goal is not so vital that it requires the hero's complete attention. There is time to explore his or her broader life and include other goals. Sub-plots can offer rest and counterpoint to the primary endeavor.

Sub-plots typically stem from the hero's work life, home life, or internal life. The woman seeking love may be dealing

POPULAR SUB-PLOTS

Hero's Work Life
Up for Promotion
Fired or put on probation
Asking for a raise
Applying for a new job
Difficulty with a coworker or boss
Assigned a difficult task

Hero's Home Life
Getting married or in a romance
A marriage breaking up
An ill relative
A delinquent relative
Raising children
A friend asks a favor
An annoying neighbor
The death of a friend

Hero's Internal Life
Physical illness or injury
Mental illness or trauma
Crisis of faith
Addiction issues
Self-esteem issues

with sick parents, trouble at work, or a crisis of religious faith. The detective hunting a killer may have a crumbling marriage due to his workaholic nature.

These secondary goals should relate thematically to the primary goal. They either add pressure to the hero's motivation, or illustrate the hero's strengths and weaknesses. For example, the sub-plot for a hero seeking treasure may relate to employment problems and money issues. In an action story, a romantic sub-plot may arm the hero with the emotional abilities he or she needs to succeed.

A word of caution: audiences have little patience for stories padded out with irrelevant sub-plots. Make sure your B- and C-stories have some relationship to the A-story.

Subordinate Characters

This structure expands the number of protagonists from one to a handful. Stories about historical events, settings, and occupations often use this structure. A famous war battle may be told from the POV of a foot soldier, a sergeant, and a general. A story set in the world of professional sports could involve players, coaches, fans, and the front office. A glimpse inside a business endeavor could involve workers on the factory floor, customers, and the CEO in her paneled office.

Subordinate characters can also mirror the hero's thematic arc, often serving a cautionary purpose. The hero may learn from another character's failure and realize what he must do to succeed.

Multiple Characters/Goals

Finally, some stories have multiple characters and goals that are loosely connected, or not connected at all. Stories based around a theme such as *War* or *Parenthood* are illustrated with an ensemble of characters involved in different

ENSEMBLE STORY TYPES

Location Based
Residents of a town or city
Of an apartment building or prison
Campers at a summer camp

Organization Based
The workers at a particular business
Aristocracy and servants in a mansion
The crew of an aircraft carrier

Endeavor Based
Commanders and soldiers in battle
Participants in a political movement
Actors putting on a show

Experience Based
Start, middle, and end of marriage
Birthing, raising, and launching children

Theme Based
Love conquers all
Crime doesn't pay

aspects of that experience. A *love* theme could involve a pair of teenagers on their first date, twenty-somethings getting married, an older couple having marital problems, and a senior dealing with the loss of a spouse.

The writer's task is to identify different aspects of their chosen setting or theme and embody them in different characters. Each plot can be outlined separately and then woven with the others. Typically the emotional arc of each thread follows the same trajectory, all reaching a *death moment* at the end of Act II and a *climax* in Act III.

CLIMAX VARIATIONS

Just as the framework of the second act is determined by the type of *endeavor*, the third act's framework stems from the *climax*. Almost all climaxes involve the direct confrontation of hero and villain, but there are a handful of variations.

The Big Event

Often a story is leading to a specific *big event*. A boxer prepares for a title match. Soldiers train for a big battle. Lovers prepare for their wedding day. The event is established early in the first or second act and the audience knows exactly where the climax is going to take place. The *death moment* may suggest the big event is off. This is often followed by a race to the climax where the resurrected hero rushes to confront the dragon or make it to the wedding.

Extra Innings

In this story type, the hero has reached their initial goal at the end of Act II. The hero, possibly a flawed person with selfish aims, has completed the minimum requirements of the *endeavor*. They are set to ride off into the sunset when it becomes apparent the villain is still a threat. They must decide to set aside their own interests and risk everything to embark on a new objective.

The Negative Ending

Sometimes heroes fail. They do not reach their goal, but have grown as a person and found a deeper purpose in life. Despite their failure, they will live on to fight another day with greater self-awareness, or have inspired others to do the same. The resonant moral of such stories is to keep trying, despite the travails of life.

The inverse is also possible. A protagonist with negative traits and habits may reach their selfish goal, only to realize they have paid a terrible personal price. Such stories serve as negative parables for the audience, warning them not to follow the same path as the protagonist.

PART FOUR

Sᴇǫᴜᴇɴᴄᴇs

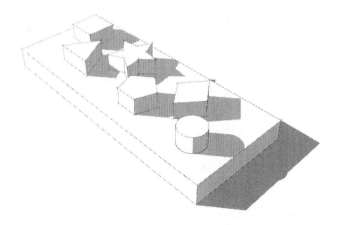

Joining Elements into Sequences

By now you have a grasp on the main elements of your story and traditional story structure. It's time to dig deeper into the process of arranging your elements in sequences.

This is where many shy away from the outlining process. Who can blame them? Much like a hero on a quest, the task shifts from fun and games to challenges and obstacles. If gathering elements is like taking photographs, designing sequences is like building a puzzle. The edge pieces are easy to assemble, but those blue "sky" pieces are sheer frustration.

Assembling the pieces of a story presents an even greater challenge. While puzzle pieces have set male-female connectors, story-elements can be tweaked and adjusted, but altering one connection impacts others, much like a Rubik's Cube.

Many writers just want to start writing. Inhabiting the world of the story is much more fun than fine-tuning structure. If you don't flesh out the design details, however, you run the risk of writing yourself into a corner or taking your characters down a blind alley. Then you would be forced to re-jigger your story, invent a solution, and laying track to justify it. Either way, you'll have to do the ugly work of designing the connections between each element.

Let's examine the main sequences of a story. We start with the most important sequence from the end of Act II to the climax.

Sequence One:
From Defeat to Victory

We know the traditional framework of this sequence:

Death Moment
Catharsis
Resurrection and New Plan
Climax

What we need to map out is how the story elements placed in this frame relate to each other. This isn't easy. There are physical requirements as well as internal thematic consider-ations. Here are some obvious connections:

--The death moment relates to the hero's goal and flaw.
--The catharsis/resurrection transcends the flaw.
--The new plan is built on the experiences of Act II.
--The climax employs the hero's new skills.

This can be a complex web of connections. Each element must fit others which in turn must fit others to build a sequence. One reason to keep things very loose in the design process is because each element may need adjusting. No element is set in stone until all elements fit tightly together. This is also why we don't bother with Act I until Acts II and III are designed. A good place to start this sequence is the hero's *flaw* and its relationship to the *death moment*.

Flaw/Failure Relationship

The *death moment* is typically the inverse of the hero's goal. Instead of winning the treasure, they lose what wealth they had. Instead of finding lasting love, the object of their desire dumps them. Instead of safely fleeing the tsunami, they are stuck in its path.

The fact the hero has failed relates to their internal flaw which guides the specific manner in which they failed. They are either doing something with flawed skills, or avoiding something due to flawed skills.

Sometimes this is a very obvious connection. In *subterfuge* stories, the *death moment* is often when the hero's deception is revealed. This lends itself to flaws relating to honesty or self-esteem. For example:

> *A hero lacking self-esteem (flaw) believes he must assume a false identity (endeavor) to win love (goal). This ruse may work for a while (fun and games), but becomes increasingly difficult to maintain (obstacles). He lacks the confidence, however, to come clean and is ultimately unmasked (Death Moment).*

There are a variety of elements in this sequence, but focus on the last sentence and how the *death moment* results from the hero's *flaw*. While the ruse could simply be revealed, it is more thematic if the hero has an opportunity to "come clean" and fails to do so. His flaw won't let him. Here's another example based on a treasure quest:

> *A hero filled with hubris (flaw) goes on a quest for treasure (goal). He succeeds in every step of the adventure (fun and games/obstacles) and is certain he can face the last challenge single-handedly. He is defeated (death moment) and only saved by the allies he's made along the way.*

In this example the hero is taking action, but that action is based on his flaw of hubris or ego. As with the previous example, there should be a decision moment. Perhaps allies

FLAW/DEATH CONNECTIONS

Dishonest	Evades Telling Truth
Lone Wolf	Rejects aide
Traumatized	Avoids facing issues
Naive	Trusts too much
Peacemaker	Tries Diplomacy
Impulsive	Charges into danger
Bitter	Acts spitefully
Selfish	Doesn't share
Timid	Doesn't speak up
Intellectual	Logic fails
Emotional	Instincts fail

FAILURE/NEW PLAN DIVISIONS

Treasure stolen	Must chase after it
Villain has weapon	Must prevent use
Delivered warning	Must fight threat
Obtain Treasure	Ally is kidnapped
Weapon broken	Devise repairs
Rescue loved one	Must flee to safety
Rescue loved one	Must rescue others
Learn target	Race to stop attack
Imprisoned	Must escape

volunteer to help him, but he rejects their assistance, believing he can reach the goal on his own.

Forming a tight bond between flaw and failure will inform a variety of other elements of your story. The next relationship to design is between failure and the new plan.

Failure/New Plan Relationship

The *flaw* influences the manner in which the hero fails at the *death moment*, but the failure itself is reversed in the *new plan*. The connections here deals with both the physical aspects of the plot and their internal relevance to the hero and the theme they represent.

Let's start with the physical. There must be a plausible manner for the hero to regroup and achieve his/her goal. On a structural level, we must have two related goals or two means to achieve the same goal. As nothing—not even your goal—is set in stone, look for a natural way in which it can be cleaved into two related parts.

The division could be one of circumstances. For example, the hero may find the treasure in Act II only to have it stolen from him by traitors. Now he must use new skills and tactics to steal it back.

The division could also be one of scale. A hero intent on saving his family from a storm, may have to save an entire village. A soldier tasked with stealing plans for a super weapon, must actually destroy that weapon.

New Skills/New Plan Relationship

Just as the hero's flaw is evident in the failure, the new plan should require that the hero consciously use the opposite kind of skills. These new skills could be the inverse of the flaw or an admirable skill the hero always possessed.

All people have good and bad qualities and just as the

hero's flaw led to defeat, her strengths and new skills lead to success. Just as the writer must cleave the physical goal in two, they must design an internal component to these actions. For example:

> *A hero who lacks self-esteem (flaw) believes he must assume a false identity (endeavor) to win love (goal). This ruse may work for a while (fun and games), but becomes increasingly difficult to maintain (obstacles). He lacks the confidence, however, to come clean and is ultimately unmasked (death moment). He has a chance to act dishonorably, but stands up for himself and this ultimately wins him love.*

In this example, the hero's flaw of low self-esteem leads to the failure. Only standing up for himself leads to his victory. How this is actively demonstrated may vary as long as it illustrates his newfound self-respect. Another example:

> *A hero filled with hubris (flaw) sets out on a quest for treasure (goal). He succeeds in every step of the venture (fun and games/obstacles) and along the way his selflessness (strength) impresses his allies. Perhaps the hero wants the treasure to fund a school for blind kids. He is certain he can face the last challenge single-handedly, but the treasure is stolen by a traitor (death moment). Inspired by the hero's selflessness, the allies work together to steal the treasure back.*

In this case the hero's strength (selflessness) inspires allies to help him. At the same time, he must give up his hubris (flaw) and work with them as a team. The goal remains the same, but the circumstances may have changed. Perhaps instead of being kept in a secure vault, the treasure is now on the move, having been stolen by a traitor. Because the location has changed, the techniques to obtain it can also change, resulting in a situation in which the hero can't work alone, but must be part of a team.

I warned you it was complex.

There are physical aspects and thematic variables within each element. Each can be adjusted, but each adjustment affects other elements. Adjust one and you may have to adjust several others.

Resurrection/Climax Relationship

This connection is comparatively easy to design. Simply look for a way in which your hero displays their *new skills* (the opposite of their *flawed skills*) in the climax.

This can be subtle or heavily underscored. A lone-wolf hero working with others is a clear demonstration of collaboration. A dishonest hero coming clean in a public setting demonstrates their honesty. A selfish hero risking his life to save others demonstrates selflessness.

The act can be further underscored by adding a moment of possible relapse. The hero may be tempted to use his flawed skills again. The audience is worried he/she will backslide. But the hero makes a conscious decision to do the right thing and it works.

Through the process of designing the defeat-to-victory sequence, you should be able to fill in the blanks of the following paragraph:

> *Because he relied on his (flaw), the hero has failed to (endeavor). Only by (catharsis) is he able to regroup and (new plan). He engages in (climax) and is tempted*

to use (flaw), but chooses (new skills) instead, thus achieving victory.

Sequence Two: Normal World to Endeavor

The second critical sequence takes your hero from their normal everyday life to the world of the *endeavor*. It's best to design this sequence after you have roughed out the failure-to-victory sequence. Knowing the components of the end make construction of the beginning much easier. We know the structural framework:

Hero's world
Hero's strengths and flaws
Hero's need
The rejection of the endeavor
Added Pressure
Embark on the endeavor.

The elements place into this framework should relate on both physical and thematic levels. As before, each element should connect tightly with those around it. The overall goal of this sequence is to motivate the hero to undertake the *endeavor*. They do this to preserve the nice life they have or improve the crummy life they currently suffer through.

Flaw/World Relationship

If all stories involve *threats* or *desires*, then the hero's life is either satisfied or frustrated. Either way, their circumstances should reflect their *flaw*. A hot-headed hero may be fired, which explains his nagging poverty. A self-centered hero may disregard the needs of her employees, which explains her wealthy-but-lonely lifestyle. Heroes seeking love should be linked to a flaw such as low self-esteem. This flaw can be dramatized through scenes that depict how it is foiling the hero's attempts to find love.

You can design this connection from either direction—world or flaw. If you have the hero's world in place, then devise how it reflects a plausible flaw. If you have a flaw in hand, look for circumstances that result from that character trait.

World/Need Relationship

The hero's day-to-day world, in turn, relates to their *need*. A poor hero seeks riches. A lonely hero seeks love. A satisfied hero craves stability. This general need doesn't initially lead to the endeavor. That happens when a specific *goal* is introduced at the *inciting incident*. Until then, heroes may engage in coping mechanisms or seek alternatives to satisfy their need.

Goal/Endeavor Relationship

The relationship between goal and endeavor is a particularly important connection to make. This relates more to the physical parameters of the story than internal themes. A *goal* is a specific means to satisfy the hero's general *need*. The *endeavor* presents the challenging means to reach it. Because you know what your endeavor is, the task is to push and pull your hero to engage in this radical course of action.

Keep in mind that some *endeavors* may not reveal their danger until later in the story. A hero could undertake the challenge unaware of its true danger until it's too late to turn back. The simplest form of goal/endeavor connection comes in the form of an assignment as part of the hero's occupation. No further motivation is required.

Examples of Pushing Your Hero

The Hero's need for money becomes critical
Added pressure from a ticking clock
Alternatives are explored and fail
Old ties are broken
Hero's safety net collapses

Examples of Pulling Your Hero

Hero's desire intensifies
The endeavor satisfies multiple goals
Peers have already accepted the challenge
Loved ones encourage him

With the previous connections in place you should be able to complete the following paragraph:

> *Due to (flaw), a hero endures (circumstances) that create a desire for (need). The hero tries to (satisfy need), but every effort proves fruitless. (Added pressure) forces the hero's hand and he reluctantly decides to (endeavor).*

With the main sequences of your story in place, all that remains to design is the specifics of the second act.

Sequence Three: The Endeavor

Now that you know where your story is going and where it started, the *endeavor* sequence should be easy to assemble. This is, after all, where much of the entertainment value of your story resides. You may already have a list of gags and set pieces in mind or mapped out the different realms your hero visits in their travels. There is only one relationship through this sequence, the link between the hero's actions and their internal growth.

Flaw/Endeavor Relationship

The thematic arc of your hero represents significant change in their character, but people don't change easily. They resist. They cope. They relapse. They fall back on old habits and flawed skills. The physical action should reflect this halting progress. Forward progress might involve the hero trying their *new skill* and having some success. Backsliding may involve the apparent failure of new skills, or the hero

Examples of Growth Steps

From Lone Wolf...

Hero succeeds with lone wolf habits
Hero rejects aide from anyone else and suffers for it
Hero discounts the helpful involvement of an ally
Hero witnesses effectiveness of a team
Hero relapses to lone-wolf ways at death moment
Hero ultimately embraces team collaboration

...to Team Player

From Selfish...

Hero acts in self interest
Others beg for generosity, but he ignores them
His philosophy is every man for himself
He suffers a blow that requires assistance
The person who aided him rejects a reward
He learns his own success was based on generosity
He rejects giving aide with tragic results
He acts selflessly to achieve goal

...to Generous

From Doubting...

Hero is told he/she is worthless
They are dismissed by everyone
Hero practices a skill in secret
He volunteers for a challenge and is mocked
He is defeated and doubts himself
He risks public ridicule and succeeds

...to Confident

doubting their effectiveness.

Make a list.

At the top of the list is your hero's *flaw*. At the bottom is the *new skill* that helps them succeed. Now design a handful of logical steps that lead from one trait to the other. Use these internal steps to help design the obstacles or subordinate goals of your second act. Obstacle may chip away at the hero's flaw. Challenges can require new skills. Every set-back can test the hero's determination.

How many steps you have may be determined by the physical action of the endeavor, the overall length of your story, or external factors. For example, a movie-studio may set the length of a movie, or a TV-network may determine the number of commercial breaks in a series episode. Fortunately, the second act can be stretched and squeezed like an accordion to whatever length is needed. Simply devise the most compelling dramatic events that chart your hero's progress.

PART FIVE

PLOT

The Plot Machine

It is time to drop a few coins in the plot machine and practice the story-design techniques we've covered. The best way to do this is to go through a few examples. The specific elements of the following stories aren't as important as the process used to design them. It boils down to this:

Create *elements* and loosely arrange them in different *frameworks*, looking for logically connected *sequences*.

Every writer has experienced the joy of having an idea burst into their heads. We have also experienced the nagging frustration of staring at a blank computer screen, waiting for the missing pieces of the story-puzzle to magically appear. Using the design process we've learned removes this frustration and offers a path through the uncharted wilderness of plot construction. This is not to say the answers will be easy to find, but half the battle is asking the right question.

Keep in mind that not every event of a story need be included in the final telling. Some things happen before the curtain rises, or off the screen or page. Think of your story as a charm bracelet. The plot is the chain that encompasses all the events of a story. The charms hanging from that chain represents the scenes you will include in the telling. You need the chain to hold everything together, but the audience will only see the pretty charms.

SLAY THE DRAGON

Every civilization has some variation on the story where a great beast imperils the village. How can the Plot Machine help design such a story? Simply ask the right questions in the right order.

What do We have?

Such stories almost always begin with the terrifying beast and that is a pretty good start. Could be a dragon, a giant robot, a alien, a shark, or some variation on that idea.

We also need a village for the beast to terrorize. The village could be a town, city, summer camp, space ship, or an entire planet. That depends on your preferred *scale*. To build audience sympathy, the village should be calm, peaceful, and idyllic. We fear its destruction.

We also have a story type: *threat*. That tells us the hero's primary goal is *safety*.

And we have elements of *scale* and *tone*. As the peril is immediate, these stories typically plays out in days or weeks, not months. The *tone* is usually serious and the *entertainment value* comes in the form of action and thrills.

What is the goal?

We know the protagonist's general need is *safety*, but that can come in various forms. The threat could be killed, but the village could also build dragon-proof defenses, or simply pack up and leave are area. Alternatives should be considered. Remember, goals have internal and external components and ideally there is a thematic relationship between the two. For now lets say the goal is to kill the dragon.

What is the endeavor?

If the goal is to kill the dragon, then the writer's task is to design a compelling *endeavor* to accomplish this.

Review the various types of *endeavors* and related *frameworks*. Is your hero on a *quest* or *storming the castle* or both? A quest story with one primary hero typically involves a series of subordinate goals. Storming the dragon's lair may require weapons, allies, and transportation.

Tone can be part of your design calculations. The adventure of a classic *quest* may seem shop-worn and familiar. A contemporary attitude with snarky humor could give a fresh tone to age-old cliches. This tone may influence the type of endeavor you choose and your hero's personality.

Let's say this is a quest story with various sub-goals.

What is the Framework of Act II?

As we consider the *endeavor*, we should also consider different framework options. Some endeavors traditionally utilize certain frameworks, but the writer should take a few minutes to experiment with different options.

This story could present a series of *obstacles* the hero must overcome to slay the dragon. Perhaps there are smaller dragons that guard a larger super-dragon. This sounds repetitions, however, and it's more likely *shifting goals* will be more interesting and entertaining.

A mid-point reversal might surprise the audience and take this familiar narrative in a fresh new direction. What would a surprising reversal be? The most extreme example would be to turn the goal on its head and have the hero team up with the dragon.

Why would the hero do this? Maybe there is a mutual enemy. Perhaps the dragon had good reason to attack the village. What would that reason be? Maybe someone in the village was harming the dragon. Maybe the dragon has laid eggs and someone in the village is stealing them? Why would someone do that? Perhaps the eggshells are made of gold.

You're a story-teller. Start exploring options.

Who is the Hero?

You'll notice we haven't discussed the hero yet. If your story-idea begins with a hero, then your next steps would be to study their environment and look for logical goals.

As this story began with the monster, we probably need a *righteous hero* or a *reluctant hero* to defeat it. The former is the village champion, a capable warrior and known dragon-killer. The latter is the lowly stable-girl, mocked by the village, and lacking both physical strength and experience.

The hero must be fit enough to undertake the quest. Tone is also a factor. If your tone is humorous, the hero should have comedic traits or a wicked sense of sarcasm.

The hero must also illustrate the universal truth you are trying to convey through their arc. The story we've devised has the hero ally himself with the dragon. This lends itself to a theme of questioning authority. As *reluctant heroes* are typically not in power, this implies our hero is more *righteous* and believes in the existing power structure.

What is the Death Moment?

Quest stories typically do not go as initially planned. The destination may be reached too late. The weapon may not work. This is where the story takes a turn, often marked by a *death moment*. What is the worst thing that could happen to our hero? How did their flaw lead to this downfall? In our story the hero's low point may be where he learns his village has been stealing eggs and the dragon's anger is justified.

What is the Climax?

We know the hero must recognize the error of his ways and embark on a new plan to reach his goal. Consider reversing the elements of the second act. Maybe traitors or enemies come to the hero's rescue. Perhaps the goal has changed. Weapons that don't work are repaired.

Our premise implies that Act III will have the hero and dragon teaming up to steal back those golden eggs and bring the thieves to justice. The very act is one of rebelling against everything the hero has come to know, demonstrating the new perspective he has learned.

What is the Framework of Act I?

With the latter elements of the story roughed out, the first act is relatively simple to design. Our theme is questioning authority, therefore we want to depict a hero at the polar opposite—one who is aligned with authority. Perhaps our hero is a prince in the realm or otherwise benefiting from family connections to the village's power structure—a structure based on greed (and stolen golden eggs).

All this should be illustrated in Act I. We need to see the hero's day-to-day world and how this world is based on a corrupt power structure. We should witness the hero's faith in that structure and rejection of any criticism. Consider subordinate characters and plots that could provide counterpoint to the hero's unquestioning faith.

WIN LOVE THROUGH TRICKERY

Subterfuge stories almost always begin with a what-if premise. What if a woman had to pass as a man, or a man as a woman? What if a servant posed as a wealthy aristocrat? What if a nobody was mistaken for a crime boss? The entertainment value comes in the audacity of the gag. This is a popular endeavor in romantic comedies as love is a great motivator for such wacky schemes. For our purposes we'll posit that a poor hero must pretend to be a rich.

What do we have?

We have a premise of poor hero pretending to be rich.

We probably also have a *desire* story in mind. *Subterfuge* is rarely an effective means to defeat a *threat*, although subterfuge can be employed to hide from one.

The goal is love and that implies a hero who lacks love in the first act.

The romantic genre implies a fantastical tone.

What is the Goal?

The general goal is love/affection/companionship. The specific goal presents itself with the inciting incident. In romantic-comedies this is often called the *meet cute* moment. Some effort is needed to design the connection between goal and endeavor. The hero could try various conventional means to connect with this love interest, but nothing works.

What is the Endeavor?

This is the central gag that probably sparked interest

in the story to begin with. Specificity matters in such fish-out-of-water stories and some thought should be given to the setting. What is the most extreme example of poor/rich contrast. Is a bum mistaken for a Wall Street tycoon? A hillbilly is mistaken for royalty. Let's say our hero is a servant working for a billionaire who is away on vacation. The inciting incident may involve mistaken identity and it's a ruse they want to sustain.

What is the Framework of Act II?

Much of the entertainment value of subterfuge stories comes in the fun and games offered at the start of Act II. The writer must design as many compelling situations as possible. These gags, however, typically can't sustain the entire second act. A mid-point reversal may serve to keep things interesting.

That reversal may come in the form of the hero achieving his/her initial goal: winning the affection of their desired mate. A milestone is crossed: a first date or a first kiss. The circumstances of the remainder of Act II are more oriented to maintaining the ruse than winning affection.

Sub-plots are helpful in such stories. There should be a handful of B- and C-level stories relating to the hero's motivation and the antagonists seeking to unmask him. The love interest may have a sub-plot of their own, explaining why they are also looking for love.

Who is the Hero?

Once again, the larger elements of the story dictate the characteristics of the hero. This is a romance, so the hero is clearly lacking love. The use of a false identity implies a theme related to honesty or self-respect. The hero may be ashamed of his/her true identity and circumstances. They believe the only way to win love is to be someone different.

The hero should be smart enough to pass themselves off as their alter-ego, but quirky enough to do so in a comedic or endearing manner. Their goal is relatable even if their means to achieve it is dishonest. To exaggerate the silliness of the gag, design a hero who is the polar opposite of what he or she must be in the second act.

What is the Death Moment?

This is easy: the hero's false identity is revealed. They may have achieved their goals, but that achievement was based on a lie. Nothing breaks the spell of love faster than a lie. Any goodwill they have earned with their romantic interest is wrecked. Even worse than losing what they have gained, is the fate of returning to their dull original life. Their old life looks even worse given the different world they've been living in.

What is the Climax?

Subterfuge stories benefit from a compelling gag, the entertainment value of fun and games, and the drama of the death moment. All this must be topped off with a satisfying resurrection and ultimate victory and this sequence is always the trickiest part of the plot.

If the *death moment* plays out the hero's flaw, then this resurrection may be based on strengths. The writer must design a plot thread that results in the hero winning love based on their positive qualities. Sub-plots are ideal for this task. Perhaps there is a B- or C-story in which the hero can secure permanent wealth by some trickery. Being an honorable person, he rejects this scheme. This so endears him to the love interest that she forgives his previous deceit and they build an honest relationship together.

What is the Framework of Act I?

The first act is largely defined by the elements we've established. The hero is seeking love, so it follows he is currently without love. Perhaps he is dumped by his current partner. We could also see the hero go through various conventional attempts to find love: singles bars, dating websites, a matchmaker, blind dates, etc. Their flaw should be evident. Perhaps they are habitual liars or exaggerators.

To justify this extreme endeavor, the motivation must 1) explain why this one particular person is the focus of the hero's infatuation, and 2) why that person will only be impressed by a rich suitor. This requires both *push* and *pull*. The pull comes in the inciting incident where the hero sees their ideal mate and is smitten. Cupid's arrow has struck hard.

The push can come in the form of a ticking clock, or a fluke opportunity that the hero spontaneously decides to take advantage of. Perhaps the love interest mistakenly assumes the butler is the billionaire, and the butler is too smitten to correct her. Once they've stepped down the road of lies, however, it is difficult to turn back.

CRIME STORY

Crime stories may be the most popular story-type in television history. The genre serves the hour-drama format well. The stories are instantly compelling, often starting with a crime, and no motivation is needed to get the hero involved in a case week after week.

A feature length crime story may require some special significance. Perhaps this is the detective's last case before retirement, or it relates to a case he never solved. Maybe the villain is targeting the detective, seeking retribution for a past conviction.

What do we have?

Crime stories typically start with the familiar genre. It can be challenging to bring something fresh to the table and that new angle often comes in the hero or setting. Maybe the hard-boiled detective is a teenager or a senior citizen. Perhaps the story is set in the old west or outer space.

The genre also tells us a lot about the overall structure. We know there will be a crime in Act I and our hero will investigate it. We know there will be clues to ponder and evidence to process. We know the entertainment value comes from puzzle-solving and perhaps some action.

What we don't have is the crime itself.

For our purposes let's say this is a routine investigation, perhaps for an hour-long television series.

What is the Goal?

Obviously, the hero wants to put the cuffs on the criminal. There are variations within the larger crime genre. The detective may know who did the crime, but lack evidence to prove it. They may have a variety of potential suspects and need to deduce which one is guilty. They may be forced to disprove the conviction of a wrongly convicted suspect.

Must of this depends on the crime itself. Detectives are reactive characters and their actions are linked to what the villain has done or is continuing to do. Let's say a murder has been committed and our hero wants to catch the killer.

What is the endeavor?

The crime genre lends itself to a *quest*. Even if the hero doesn't leave their city, they must explore hidden aspects of it. The hero's journey is more intellectual than geographic. This is a *treasure* story, but the reward is putting the criminal behind bars and gaining the satisfaction of restoring balance to the imbalance of an unpunished crime.

As the dogged pursuit of clues and evidence can grow tedious, some key turning points should be established. The first turning point typically raises the stakes for the hero. Often another body is found, implying a serial killer is on the loose. Alternatively, there could be some link to a past case, or a macabre pattern to the crimes.

What is the Framework of Act II?

Detective stories are typically filled with one nagging obstacle: the lack of information. While the main goal is arresting the criminal, numerous subordinate goals may be involved, each linked to a piece of information. Who is the victim? Where is the murder weapon? Are their any witnesses?

One way to fill the second act is to take away as much information from the hero as possible. Perhaps there is no identification on the body. Perhaps there is no body. If there are witnesses, they aren't talking. There is no murder weapon.

The cause of death baffles the medical examiner. Give your hero as little as possible to go on.

The hero should stub their toe with each step of their investigation. Information does not come easy and only leads to more questions. Rules may need to be bent or broken. Subplots can serve as counterpoint to the investigation. These may involve the detective's home life or personal life.

Who is the Hero?

Most crime stories involve qualified detectives with skills that justify the position they hold. Often they are *righteous heroes*, though the film-noir genre adds flaws like addiction, greed, or a callous disregard for others.

Detectives are often imbued with extraordinary investigative skills. The entertainment value comes from having such champion puzzle-solvers initially stumped by a perplexing scenario. Detectives often have no growth arc. They end the investigation much as they began it.

To that end, the writer has to treat the villain as the main character and map out their motivations, goals, plans, and complications. The detective must then unravel these elements through sleuthing. This relationship between the hero's front story and the villain's background story can be challenging to design. Foreground detective work must logically relate to the villain's unseen activities.

What is the Death Moment?

The tension of a crime story comes in the frustrating lack of information. The release comes when nagging questions are answered. The *death moment* can result from this friction. An arrest could be made, but the hero believes it's the wrong perpetrator. The criminal could be arrested, but the case tossed out due to the hero's aggressive tactics.

This turning point is a major set-back to the case, but it should be noted that detectives have little personal stake in solving the crime other than to seek justice.

What is the Climax?

In crime stories, the climax is where the hero identifies and apprehends the criminal. These events can be in close proximity or some distance apart. One final piece of evidence typically leads to this event and that key information is only obtained through the hero's exceptional skills.

As intellectual exercises, crime stories often involve false leads and misdirections employed to trick the hero (and the audience). In turn, the hero may employ tricks to trip-up the villain. This is another reason why crime stories require the design of the villain's story as much as the hero's.

What is the Framework of Act I?

In this genre, there often isn't a first act at all. Given that the hero doesn't change much internally, there is no need to see him in his normal world. Crime stories often begin with the detective arriving on the scene. In feature-length stories, some common investigative steps may happen in Act I. Who is the victim? What is their backstory? Who were their enemies? How was the crime done? What is the physical evidence? Only when the case takes on a special significance do we make the turn into the *endeavor*.

It is the writer's job to establish something particularly compelling about this case. There should be a perplexing element that challenges even our detective's vaunted skills. Perhaps the body was found in a room locked from the inside. Maybe the crown jewels were stolen from an impregnable safe. Establishing a particular intellectual puzzle will hook the audience and draw them through the investigation.

PERSONAL GOAL STORY

Not all hero's are trying to slay a dragon or catch a serial killer. Some just want to accomplish a personal goal. It might be climbing a mountain, graduating from college, or going the distance with the heavyweight champion of the world. We all set goals, some impossibly high, and inspiring stories of achievement can spur us to face our own challenges.

What Do We Have?

Such stories often start with the challenge itself. Perhaps it is the world of marathon runners, professional poker players, or a famous event like the Tour de France, National Spelling Bee, or a talent competition. The entertainment value comes in the vicarious experience of entering this unique world.

The big event may give us the second act *endeavor* or the third act *climax* depending on the scale of the story and particulars of the event. The Tour de France lasts for weeks and could consume the second act. A boxing match would more likely occupy the third act, with the second act devoted to preparation.

Let's posit that our hero is training to run a marathon.

What is the Goal?

Our hero's goal is known early in Act I or Act II. There is no pressing threat nor is there a tangible treasure. Accomplishing the feat is the tangible goal, but the real reward is the intangible sense of accomplishment and self-worth. Through the story, we learn that the emotional reward of reaching this goal takes on more and more importance.

What is the Endeavor?

This is naturally a *prepare for battle* story. As our hero prepares for a marathon, they are training and running in preliminary races. The writer's task is to design a group of obstacles related to skills the hero needs to succeed. Soldiers learn battle tactics and how to use weapons. Our marathon runner will train his/her body to build strength and stamina.

What is the Framework of Act II?

Training alone may not be enough to sustain a full-length story. The writer should consider subordinate goals that relate to the goal. Our marathon runner may need to recruit a coach or mentor. There may be a key challenger. The hero may need equipment and the funds for shoes and travel expenses.

Subplots should relate to the hero's decision. Look at the race as a pebble in a pond creating waves through every aspect of the hero's personal, professional, and internal life. There are a steady stream of naysayers happy to mock our hero as he/she makes slow progress toward the big race.

Who is the Hero?

In this story, the hero is largely defined by the universal truth the writer hopes to illustrate. This story lends itself to themes of self-worth, triumph of the human spirit, and rising above adversity. Each theme would merit variations in the design of the hero.

Maybe our marathon runner is older and grasping at a last gasp of youth. Maybe he's overweight and running is part of a goal to regain fitness. Maybe she is dealing with a disability and wants to prove she can rise above it. An aging athlete may embody the value of experience. A maligned amateur could symbolize the power of self-confidence.

As this endeavor is difficult, our hero is probably not a

professional marathon runner. The hero must have some abilities, however, and the story of an unlikely, even unqualified, runner can have deep resonance.

What is the Death Moment?

The death moment relates to the marathon, but has more internal than external resonance. Perhaps the hero didn't make the cut in a qualifying race. It appears their dream is over. They suffer the reactions of the naysayers and doubt themselves. Conversely, they could double-down on what appears to be an impossible dream. Perhaps they quit their job to train full time. The act may end with personal relationships and professional status in peril.

What is the Climax?

We have known all along that the climax will be the marathon. This competition may take place in a new geographic location. The hero has risen from his death moment—perhaps another athlete suffered an injury, thus creating a spot for our hero in the race. Often an inspirational story will have a mixed ending in which the hero fails at the tangible goal, but succeeds in satisfying their need for self-esteem. They may not win the race, but win the respect of the community. The denouement depicts their self-esteem and respect.

What is the Shape of Act I?

It is important to view an inspirational hero in his/her real-world environment. We want to appreciate their strengths and weaknesses and also put in place the various sub-plots impacted by their decision to run a marathon. Chief among these elements are the various doubters, the allies the hero will need, and the personal and professional relationships that will be tested.

A GREAT REALM STORY

Some stories are told on an epic landscape. The individual characters and their goals serve to depict the spectacle of this great realm. Writers love to create such worlds and readers enjoy immersing themselves in different lands or universes.

What Do We Have?

Epic stories often start with a setting, one that may exist in great detail in the writer's mind. The setting could be geographical, institutional, or historical.

Much of the entertainment value comes in the exploration of this setting. That implies a *quest* to new lands filled with scenery, action, and thrills.

The scope of such stories could be vast, spanning great stretches of time and geography. If the goal is to explore the far reaches of this realm, then we must have a story that takes the audience hither and yon. This will likely involve several protagonists from different corners of the region.

What we don't have is a *threat* or *desire* that serves as the spine for this exploration. As scale is part of our entertainment value, we need a premise that is BIG.

What is the Goal?

This could be a *treasure* story, with a hero or heroes on a journey to obtain riches. *Treasure* stories rarely involve the masses, however, and we want a sprawling story. *Threat* stories can involve every citizen of a realm. The general goal is safety and the restoration of peace and stability.

To design the *goal*, we need to design the *threat*. One dragon attacking a village isn't enough. We want a story that explores the social and political make-up of the whole land. Perhaps the King has died without an heir, throwing the realm into civil war. Perhaps a terrible evil has arisen that can only be defeated by the collaboration of a disparate group of unlikely warriors. The specific goal could start modestly.

Let's say our heroes want to spread the word that an invading army is poised to attack.

What is the Endeavor?

As this is a *quest*, the design of our *endeavor* revolves around the destination and the obstacles in the way. Our hero's want to raise the alarm so the local army can defeat the invaders. This local army could be several obstacles away. The obstacles could be features of the landscape such as mountains, rivers, and chasms. They could be man-made in the form of traitors and spies.

What is the Framework of Act II?

Sprawling stories typically involve a group of heroes, each with their own personal goals and back stories. It can be helpful to establish subordinate goals and design the major turning points of the story.

The second act will likely begin with a primary hero embarking on the sensible goal of raising the alarm. The fun and games section of the story could involve the introduction of allies and surviving various obstacles.

A mid-point reversal can mark the end of the initial goal and beginning of a new one. Perhaps our heroes deliver the warning, but it falls on deaf or traitorous ears. This could motivate the heroes to carry their warning on to others, or to engage in alternatives such as building defences or fleeing to safety. These shifting goals should become increasingly difficult and dangerous.

The quest may only be part of the larger tapestry. An epic narrative can jump around from one location and story line to another, all linked by the mounting evil and the heroes' attempts to stop it. Each hero's story line could be plotted separately then shuffled together. Don't forget the villain. He or she has a master plan and is moving pieces on their game-board. These moves may serve to spark the heroes' reaction.

Who is the Hero?

Epic stories typically involve several heroes and perhaps several villains. The protagonists want to fend off the invasion and restore peace. The antagonists want to upset the current power structure for their own gain.

Each character has their own backstory, flaw, strengths and story-arc. Each should serve to explore a different aspect of the realm. The heroes could be equally weighted or there may be one or two—often a mentor and novice—that are more prominent.

Epic stories often require people from different back-grounds to work together. This collaboration supports themes of shared sacrifice and looking beyond your own tribe. Each character should embodied a positive or negative aspect of this thematic terrain.

What is the Death Moment?

Clearly, the heroes fail in their attempt to raise the defend-ing army. Either they could not deliver their message, it was ignored, or the resulting preparations are too little too late. The death moment could mark not only their failure, but the villain's apparent success as the invasion begins. Given that there are several protagonists and antagonists, each story line should be designed and arranged so the various death moments occur in close proximity to one another.

What is the Climax?

Things are bleak for the heroes. They may have sustained losses and are gasping for breath. The weaker among them flee and beg the others to follow.

A new plan is needed, something to snatch victory from defeat. The heroes must embark on an even bolder endeavor. They initially wanted to merely warn others, but now must engage in battle themselves.

The writer's task is to design a sequence that connects the events of Act II with a plausible new plan for Act III. Perhaps the hero's have learned about a weakness in the villain's army or plan of attack. Maybe they know what sort of weaponry or tactics will work effectively. For example, they could know the invaders are marching through a narrow mountain chasm and plan to start an avalanche that will block the way.

This plan should relate to the dominant themes of the story, such as the benefits of collaboration and steadfastness in the face of great odds. The skills and self-awareness each hero picks up along the way aids them in their victory.

What is the Shape of Act I?

We want to see each hero's normal world. We want to care about it and its survival. The writer can indulge their imagination with creative scenic detail. The introduction of the army presents an obvious *inciting incident*.

Often epic stories have a slow-burn quality to their first act. The intrigue by the villain is subtle and slow to manifest. Heroes may respond tentatively and in half-measures, coping to sustain their normal existence, rather than risking everything on a desperate journey.

Don't forget the villain. Their actions likely spark the *inciting incident* and send the heroes on their adventure.

PART SIX

WRITING

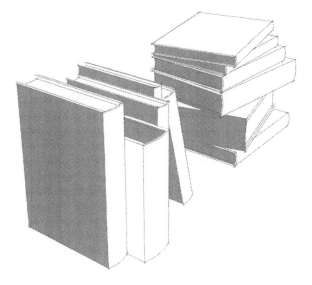

Design and Writing

This is a design guide, not a writing guide, but the ultimate execution of any design hovers over the entire process. Architects know their plans will eventually be built. Cement will be poured. Steel will be welded. Wood timbers will be nailed together. Their marks on paper will become a physical thing that people will inhabit.

Likewise, writers should be aware of writing and marketing their stories even as they design them. External factors can exert a heavy influence on design. Our creative muse is weighted by practical considerations of audience expectations, deadlines, and market forces.

Even independently published writers, unbeholden to any publisher's schedule or editor's scrutiny, should consider the meta-issues of story design. Do you have time to write an epic novel? Will your established readers migrate to a new series? Should you write shorter works to generate more titles faster? What is the competition doing?

Design is inevitably wrapped up in writing and marketing. Fortunately, solid design skills can help with these larger issues. Writers may be especially well-suited to view a process from every possible angle. After all, our art is the process of taking events and arranging them into meaningful sequences.

As you design keep the following external issues in the back of your mind.

Writing Style

Every writer has a unique voice and style. How you write should be lurking in the back of your mind as you design a story. Perhaps you are a master of poetic description. Allow room for that in your design. Maybe you're great at character and lively dialogue. Make room for that as well.

Just as every writer brings something unique to their telling, every story can present different challenges. An epic tale would probably utilize a third-person narrator, but a gritty crime story may be told in first-person. Some narrators are objective while others have sharp personalities and biased agendas. As you design, keep in mind who will be telling your story.

Just as important is how the story will be told. Is your narrator reflecting on historic events, or describing an adventure as it happens? Will your story be told in a linear sequence, or will the narrative skip around in time, location, and perspective? A well-designed story can be told in a number of ways.

Who is your Audience?

We write to be read. Who is doing that reading? Knowing your customer is perhaps the most important external factor of design. I use the word *customer* with some hesitation. We like to call the people who read our work *readers* or *fans* and take the commerce out of the equation entirely. But they are also customers who will not only invest their time in your story, but their money as well.

Writing for the market is as frowned upon as the over-reliance on structure. Authors are supposed to exist on a higher plane of creativity, and any commercial quality of their work is an unintended and surprising coincidence. At least that is the image favored by traditional publishers and creative writing programs.

The reality is we have to eat just like everyone else. And a new car every few years is a nice thing. To that end, keep your customers in mind. This is easier than ever with a vibrant presence on the internet. Work to find the balance between what you love to write and what a good number of readers love to read.

Genre or Literary?

Human beings are habitual organizers. When you tell someone you're a writer, they will immediately ask, "What do you write?" They want to know your genre. Crime? Romance? Science Fiction? Childrens? Of course, writers are just as guilty of asking readers, "What do you read?"

The rise of online sales has resulted in an increasingly sub-divided marketplace. Entire new genres such as Young Adult and Steamy Romance have been carved out of the literary firmament. There doesn't seem to be an end to the micro-categories a novel can be assigned to. Much of this is practical. Retailers need a means to organize the millions of novels being uploaded every year and readers need a system to locate other works similar to the story they just enjoyed.

As you design your story, keep in mind the process by which is will be filed, sorted, and labeled. Some authors take advantage of this by intentionally writing for obscure or trending categories. Others are stymied by a process that has no place for their genre-bending work. Either way, be aware of the categories in which your work will be placed.

Solo or Series?

Our personal-media world has forever changed the process of marketing books, movies, and television. There is no easy way to reach an audience that no longer reads the same newspapers or watches the same handful of TV networks.

Just as novels have been categorized, the audience for them has been fractured and sub-divided. Publishers, movie studios, and television networks all recognize that marketing to such a diffuse audience is expensive. The preferred solution is to create franchise entertainment where one movie or novel leads to another and another.

Independent authors have also adopted this practice. Building an audience for a series is easier than marketing solo works. This is not to say that writers should abandon the solo novel, just that they should be aware of the marketing challenges inherent to one-off titles.

Marketing

Did I mention writers have to eat? We do. And more than just macaroni and cheese. This means selling our work and that means marketing. Again this touches upon the crass world of commerce. In an ideal world, a writer's unique voice finds a suitable audience and both live happily every after. And that audience need not be large. Ten thousand readers paying five-bucks a year for your latest novel isn't a bad income. People have lived on a lot less.

Building that audience may take time. It may also take a consistent product, either a series involving the same heroes and setting, or solo works within the same genre. Marketing also requires obvious things like a compelling title and cover art. As you design your story, keep an eye out for a logical title that sparks the imagination. Look for a compelling visual that distills the essential conflict of your story. In the movie business, this is called the poster image. Often this is the hero engaged in the fun-and-games portion of the story.

Final Thoughts

We live stories. Every new day presents a new set of goals, the endeavors to reach them, and the obstacles that stand in our way. My own endeavor of writing this guide was to reach a specific goal: a process to design better stories faster.

At some point a writer must stop designing and start writing. Every writer will mark this transition differently. Some will take the main sweeps of a story and dive into prose. Others will create beat-sheets outlining each chapter and scene.

The transition need not be definite or permanent. If outlining sparks a compelling scene, go ahead and sketch it out. If the writing isn't going well, check your outline and see if it needs adjusting.

Hopefully, the process of designing from general to specific and asking the right questions in the right order will result in more efficient writing and less writer's block. There should be no further need to stare at the blank page or computer screen, waiting for lightning to strike.

Designing a story is simply a process of gathering elements and arranging them in sequences. Part of writing is collecting the elements and sequences we see in the world around us. Newspaper and magazine articles are good sources of *goals* and *endeavors*. As you watch movies and television shows, make a conscious effort to identify the framework and sequences the screenwriter has created.

Make lists of elements. Study them. Develop the mental muscles needed to arrange parts and customize their connections to other parts. Think in sequence. Start with Act II.

Good luck.

Now start designing.

The Plot Machine

From Blank Page...

What do you have?
What are natural extensions?
What is the Entertainment Value?
Consider Scale, Tone, and Theme.
Identify the General Goal.
Experiment with different Endeavors.
Experiment with Act II Framework.
Obstacles or Sub-Goals?
Do you need a Midpoint Reversal?
What is the Death Moment?
Design a Hero to fit these Elements.
Identify their strengths and flaws.
Design the Failure to Success Sequence.
Design the World to Endeavor Sequence.
Break the hero's Growth Arc into steps.
Link these steps to the Endeavor.
Design the hero's Normal World.
Link hero's Flaw to their Circumstances.
Link Circumstances to Need.
Link Need to Goal with Inciting Incident.
Link Goal to Endeavor.

...to Story

Classic Story Structure

ACT I
Hero's World
Strengths and Flaw
Hero's Need
Logical Solutions
The Inciting Incident
Rejecting the Endeavor
Added Pressure

ACT TWO
Begin the Endeavor
Fun and Games
Shifting Goals
Allies and Obstacles
Mid Point Reversal
Complications and Set-Backs
Death Moment

ACT III
Catharsis and Resurrection
A New Plan
Race to the Climax
The Climax
Denouement

About the Author

Writer Dale Kutzera worked as a screenwriter for over ten years. He is a recipient of the Carl Sautter Screenwriting Award, the Environmental Media Award, and participated in the Warner Brother Writers Workshop. He writes about writing and filmmaking at www.DaleKutzera.com.

His novels include *Manhunt* and the middle-grade adventures *Andy McBean and the War of the Worlds* and *Andy McBean 20,000 Leagues Under the Sea.*

If you enjoyed *The Plot Machine* please tell your friends and post a review online at Amazon and Goodreads.

Made in the USA
Lexington, KY
13 December 2016